*Dedicated to the people of Padstow who, in the early 1960s, inspired me without knowing it to follow good fellowship and celebrations, and unite with the true people's culture of music, dance and song of these islands.*

# MayDay

## The Coming of Spring

### Doc Rowe

ENGLISH HERITAGE

Published by English Heritage,
Isambard House, Kemble Drive, Swindon SN2 2GZ
**www.english-heritage.org.uk**

English Heritage is the Government's statutory adviser
on all aspects of the historic environment.

© Doc Rowe 2006

Every effort has been made to trace copyright holders and we apologise in
advance for any unintentional omissions, which we would be pleased to
correct in any subsequent edition of this book.

First published 2006

ISBN-10  1 85074 983 3
ISBN-13  978 1 85074 983 7
Product code  51181

*British Library Cataloguing in Publication Data*
A CIP catalogue record for this book is available from the British Library.

Edited and brought to press by Adèle Campbell
Designed by Peter Bailey
Printed by Bath Press

FRONT COVER  *Padstow May Day celebrations*
OPPOSITE TITLE PAGE  *Jack-in-the-Green, Hastings*
TITLE PAGE  *Iffley May Day procession, photographed by Henry Taunt, 1906*

# CONTENTS

INTRODUCTION                          6

MAY DAYS                              8

MAY GARLANDS                         36

PADSTOW 'OBBY 'OSS DAY               38

MINEHEAD HOBBY HORSE                 44

HUNTING THE EARL
OF RONE                              46

HASTINGS JACK-IN-
THE-GREEN                            50

HELSTON FLORAL DANCE                 52

BARWICK-IN-ELMET
MAYPOLE                              56

ABBOTSBURY GARLANDS                  58

GROVELY FOREST
RIGHTS                               60

CASTLETON
GARLAND DAY                          64

DERBYSHIRE WELL
DRESSING                             68

WHITBY PENNY HEDGE                   70

BEATING THE BOUNDS,
TOWER OF LONDON                      72

BEATING THE BOUNDS,
ST MICHAELS, OXFORD                  74

BREAD AND CHEESE DOLE,
ST BRIAVELS                          76

COOPER'S HILL,
CHEESE ROLLING                       78

COTSWOLD OLYMPICS                    82

CORBY POLE FAIR                      84

BAMPTON MORRIS                       86

CALENDAR OF MAY
EVENTS                               90

SELECTED READING                     94

# INTRODUCTION

Just as our Christmas traditions were fashioned to a great extent by Victorian sentimentality, so too has the month of May, with its portrayals of Merrie England, been 'adjusted' through the ages. Though May has a great number of traditions and customs, most are no longer of any communal or social significance and are therefore generally not as well known as those of Christmas, which are still focused largely on the family. For convenience, many May Day activities have now been moved to the new May Day holiday (or Saturday nearest). Similarly, Ascensiontide and Whit Monday events have been transferred to the late Spring Bank Holiday. But long before any official May bank holidays the year was marked out by special days: whether they were rent days, hiring fairs or customary events, they all measured the passing year. These were days to celebrate, days when people would do, eat or make things they wouldn't normally do.

May marks the end of the harsh winter and the beginning of the bright, productive summer months. For our ancestors, largely in rural areas, it was the major annual festival and was celebrated throughout the country, especially on the first of May, with music, dancing and games. A central element of May Day festivities today continues to be people 'partying' or 'celebrating themselves', whether a whole town or village, a micro community or family group. Their festivities can be as small and disregarded as the Whitby Penny Hedge ceremony, or as huge and remarkable as Padstow's May Day.

Ideas and beliefs of the origins of May Day are varied. The richness and variety of British traditions is sometimes surprising and it is often too easy to ignore the effect of exposure to centuries of overseas' influence. We know, for instance, that the Romans held Floralia celebrations and it is thought that May

Day could have its origin in this ancient festival dedicated to Flora, the goddess of fruit and flowers. Certainly in Celtic Britain, the festival of Beltane (on the eve of May Day) celebrated the coming spring and its associations of new growth and fertility. A key point of the agricultural year, Beltane – meaning 'bright fire' – was marked with night-time bonfires and animal sacrifices to the sun god. In later centuries people would celebrate by dancing round the fires and would walk, or leap, through the dying embers for luck – not forgetting to drive their cattle through as well. Incidentally, in both Scotland and Ireland it was thought risky to give fire from one's home on May Day. The lighting of such fires was still common in Scotland until about 160 years ago and in Wales up to the beginning of the 20th century. Fire sites are recalled in place names like Tan-y-bryn (fire-hill), in Carmarthenshire.

The aim of this book is to introduce the reader to, and celebrate, the rich May Day heritage that exists in the British Isles and to give a guide to some events that may be visited and supported. I hope it will provide enjoyment and some surprises but it includes a plea on behalf of the communites featured: that visitors respect their celebrations and behave appropriately. These events have emotional and demonstrative significance that is seriously upheld; they are, mostly, not staged as tourist attractions and have in some cases survived despite external pressures.

I hope the book may also go some way to say 'thank you' to the many people and communities thoughout the UK that have allowed me the privilege of sharing their very special days.

*Doc Rowe, 2006*

# MAY DAYS

Our knowledge of earlier May Day celebrations derives from diary entries, churchwardens' accounts, police and court records, usage of seasonal references by poets and writers and more specific written attacks on behaviour and morals, usually by the clergy. Writers, poets, teachers, reformers, religious and political groups, fête organisers and breweries, not forgetting milkmaids, chimney sweeps, Catholics, socialists and the Band of Hope, have all embraced the standard vision of May celebrations through the ages. Their connection is generally nostalgic, however, and even today references to this popular festival generally hark back to earlier writings, thus fostering the assumption that these events are all ancient and therefore 'pagan'.

In 1817 Squire Mason of Necton, Norfolk, initiated a 'traditional' Whit Monday celebration that included a maypole, with a dozen children 'performing a set dance about it, and maskers or Morris dancers, fancifully attired'. In 1821, Horace Smith appealed for the revival of May Day as a national festival to epitomise a 'cheerful and cordial intercourse with nature'. In 1833 Tennyson published *The May Queen* and nine years later George Daniel published *Merrie England in the Olden Time*, with a clear enthusiasm to revive the 'festivals of medieval times', as he saw them advocating the maypole as the key symbol of 'social unity and harmony'. Almost certainly influenced by his writing, there were soon a great number of tableaux featuring maypoles, May queens and Morris dancers at fêtes and London theatres. In fact, it is almost certain that the plaited-ribboned maypole first appeared in J T Haines's play *Richard Plantagenet* at the Victoria Theatre, London, in 1836. This form of display was seen at a Buxton well-dressing ceremony in 1840 and within ten years it was familiar in the south of England with a 'Tudor May game' held at Crystal Palace in 1850. In Chesire, at Arley Hall, a celebration featuring a coronation of a May queen with maypole dancing was held until 1866. It was this event that was to be 'adopted' by others. A committee from Knutsford in Cheshire, added historical characters as well Morris dancers and a Jack-in-the Green to their crowning ceremonies in the 1860s and created one of the biggest and most organised of the May processions, which was a mixture of practically every element of a 'typical' May Day. We have records of a girl 'Queen' at

*'Wake me early in the morning, Mother!' A magic lantern slide to accompany Tennyson's* The May Queen.

Avington in Berkshire, as early as 1815, and another in 1833 at Albrighton, Shropshire; but it was the Cheshire ceremonies that were the major influence and vogue. By the 1890s May queens were being crowned everywhere. Additionally, these coronations inspired the creation of 'Rose Queens' during the mid-summer months, and 'Harvest Queens' at the appropriate season.

None other than John Ruskin, a passionate advocate of the values of the Middle Ages, who had witnessed the Cheshire events, devised a May Queen ceremony in 1881 complete with a ribboned Maypole dance. This ceremony at Whiteland's, a Church of England teacher training college for women in Chelsea, London, was the ceremony that the teachers were to propagate – in whatever school they taught in throughout the world. In the 1880s, musician and pageant-master Richard D'Arcy Ferris (or de Ferrers) created 'medieval' summer games in Cheltenham: unable to find any appropriate material from the 15th century, he simply devised a glorious array that included Morris dancers, lords of misrule, hobby horses, mummers, wassailers and Highland Scottish dances. He later toured his own Morris troupe, with costumes derived from the images on a stained-glass window at Betley Hall in Staffordshire. His was unquestioningly accepted as an authentic tradition and was copied extensively. In 1887 the troupe was presented at Gray's Inn for Victoria's Golden Jubilee. Interestingly, within ten years the hobby horse became firmly accepted as an essential, historical, part of the Morris dance itself.

But happened before the reign of the May Queens?

## ANCIENT MAY CELEBRATIONS
Natural forces were thought to be so powerful on May Day that a number of charms and traditions arose to combat or control them. For instance, in the North of England it was thought that dairy production could be affected and

it was widely believed that animals were easily bewitched on this day. To counter this, a sprig of rowan or a holed stone would be placed outside stable doors. Fishermen have many May Day superstitions. Fenland fishermen would never push their boats out on this day as they might see the ghosts of their dead colleagues. In Sussex, however, the first catch on May Day brought good luck and the fishermen garland their masts on this day. But broom-makers worked on May Day, 'for to turn a branch into a broom on this day was very unlucky'.

May Eve was known as Mischief Night in some regions (although in the North of England this fell on 4th November) and all sorts of practical jokes were played and a general nuisance made. Horns would be blown in the middle of the night and tin-can bands would awaken sleepers.

Reports of this licensed misrule are plentiful. An 1895 report from Derbyshire tells that this is the night when 'youths throw bricks down chimneys, pull gates off their hinges, and do all kinds of wanton mischief' but, it adds, 'if you hang a brush, shovel, or broom outside your house, the mischief makers will pass by your house and do no harm'. In the 17th century John Aubrey wrote of boys that 'do blow cows horns and hollow caxes all night' and 'the young maids of every parish carry about their parish Garlands of Flowers, which afterwards they hang up in their churches'.

In many country districts May morning, or the eve of May Day, saw young people spending the night gathering flowering branches, bushes and greenery to decorate their houses. At one time it was also popular to go out before sunrise on May Day to collect dew in the belief it could remove blemishes and freckles. It was also supposed to be a cure for consumption and is still thought to be effective in easing rheumatism. This practice is mentioned in Samuel Pepys' Diary in 1667, and there is an earlier record of Henry VIII and his wife,

Catherine of Aragon, riding out of Greenwich Palace on May Day 1515 to gather Maydew and feast in the woods of Shooter's Hill. Subsequent monarchs were not so enthusiastic and under Elizabeth I the custom was attacked as 'empty frivolity, carrying a risk of debauchery'.

In the North West and the Midlands, between sunset and dawn, May birchers would go on their rounds secretly fixing greenery to people's houses. Each branch or spray was carefully chosen by the birchers so that its name rhymed with whatever they considered to be the most outstanding character or quality of the householder they visited. Pear rhymes with fair, lime wih prime, but briar, holly and plum stood respectively for liar, folly and glum. In Cheshire, a branch of alder pronounced 'owler' signified a scowler. Hawthorn in flower was a compliment but any other thorn was seen as 'scorn'. Nettles, thistles crab-apples, nettles and weeds may have had a more direct association.

In the North of England, particularly Lancashire, May 1st was a kind of late April Fool's Day when all sorts of pranks would take place. 'May Gosling' was the shout if you managed to trick someone, but more fool you if you tried this after midday, when the response would be 'May Goslings past and gone. You're the fool for making me one!'

Many plants were considered unlucky. Black sycamore and ash were disliked in Cornwall, rowan and birch were frowned upon in Scotland and Wales and it was generally felt inadvisable to bring into the house any whitethorn, blackthorn, elder, broom, alder, furze or snowdrops.

In many English villages children would play truant – with permission – and parade with garlands of flowers, sometimes fastened to sticks in the shape of a cross or fixed to hoops, all done in the hope of collecting money. This was sometimes known as May Dolling after the practice of placing a small doll in the centre of the garland. Variously described as the 'Virgin Mary', 'Flora'

*Abbotsbury Garland, Dorset*

and the 'May Queen', the doll was hidden in the garland itself or in a decorated box covered with greenery. Frequently there was a garland song that begged for pennies and householders were asked if they wished to see the May Doll or Queen. If they did, the doll would be uncovered and the bearer would expect a coin or gift.

Samuel Pepys noted seeing the Milkmaids' Garland in Leadenhall Street, London, on May Day 1663. Four years later he encountered some more near Drury Lane, 'with their garlands upon their pails, dancing with a fiddler before them'.

May Day was also observed as the chimney sweeps' holiday and they too would parade through the streets. It became quite usual to see the milkmaids

*Milkmaids and their garlands of plate*

and the sweeps in procession with each other. By the end of the century, instead of dancing with their pails the maids 'wore' a pyramid of light wood on their heads covered in ribbons, flowers and borrowed silver plate. Descriptions a century later say they were also joined by 'bunters' – the women who picked rags in the city. A painting of the milkmaids' garland in the Victoria and Albert Museum shows milkmaids dancing, accompanied by two chimney sweeps and a peg-leg fiddler.

Garland ceremonies continue today. At Bampton in Oxfordshire, the Spring Bank Holiday marks the beginning of the traditional Morris Dance season and in the morning children bring out a selection of garlands, some with May Dolls.

This practice wasn't restricted to the green and pleasant rural landscape; there are accounts of industrial 'garlanding' using ribbons in Manchester and Preston, where there was a deficiency of foliage, and in the Black Country a cry would be heard 'Waken chaps and wenches gay; I'm off t'country to gather May'. Fishermen in Sussex would put to sea with a garland tied to their mast on this day. At Devonport, a replica of an old-style boat resting on garlands of flowers was carried aloft from the dockyards in procession to the accompaniment of a band. This Millbrook procession bore garlands and collected money. This ceremony was revived briefly a few years ago. In Whitby, North Yorkshire, better known for its fishing industry, the day was known as Horse Ribbon Day and saw stablemen and drayman on May Day decorating their horses with ribbons which they had first begged from local shops. The horse, apart from being the main working animal on the land, has always been a potent symbol of strength and virility, and is the focus of a number of May Day festivities.

## THE MODERN MAY

Though times, beliefs and communities have changed since the fires of Beltane, there is today no shortage of May events and festivities across the country. Six o'clock on May morning sees the choristers of Magdalen College Chapel, Oxford, assemble at the top of the tower to sing *Te deum Patrem Colimus*, a hymn of thanksgiving written in 1660. Despite the early hour spectators turn out to hear the singing and see the many Morris Dancers in the city streets, adding the sound of their bells to those of the chapel. The public houses are open from 6.30 in the morning and many people stay up all night drinking. Many are willing to jump from Magdalen Bridge into the not-so-deep River Chewell; a traditional activity of course. A similar ceremony – Singing on the Bargate – is held at sunrise in Southampton by the choristers of King Edward VI School and in a number of places throughout England, Morris men dance in the May dawn.

Thousands of people gather in Padstow in Cornwall every May Day to see the two famous Hobby Horses, the 'Old 'Oss' and 'Blue Ribbon 'Oss'. There is a communal build-up to the celebrations weeks before, then just before midnight on 30th April the Padstow people assemble outside the Golden Lion Inn, the stable of the Old 'Oss. At the stroke of midnight they start unaccompanied singing the Night Song: 'Unite and unite, and let us all unite. For the summer is acome unto day…' After serenading the landlord and landlady the Mayers move on through the town, singing – with occasional stops at other pubs – until the very early hours.

In the early morning a number of children's 'osses – known as colt 'osses – cavort around the town then at 10.00 am a huge band of drummers, melodeon and accordion players, led by a resplendent master of ceremonies, greets the Blue Ribbon 'Oss. It is coaxed on by a 'teaser' – a Mayer brandishing a decorated club; the crowd is emotional, overjoyed to see the 'Oss after a 12-month wait. After a number of individuals have taken a turn in the teasing the 'Oss moves off around the town. One hour later the Old 'Oss leaves its stable at The Golden Lion, similarly accompanied, terrifying some of the visitors and animals with its frenetic dancing. The two 'Osses and their supporters take different routes through the town until they meet under the maypole in Broad Street and dance together, then blue ribbons and red intermingle for the rest of the day.

Stories abound of the origins of this tradition and a common one is the 'Oss being used to frighten invaders away from our shores. During the siege of Calais in the 14th century, when the Padstow men were away fighting the French, a French warship appeared at Stepper Point and the local women are said to have dressed themselves in red cloaks and walked, with the 'Oss in front, along the cliff top. Thinking the militia had arrived with the devil at its head, the French promptly sailed away.

16

Further along the coast, at Minehead in Somerset, the Sailor's Hobby Horse tradition has fewer visitors than Padstow's but is no less dramatic. This horse is a hessian-covered wooden frame carried on a dancer's shoulders, rather like an upturned boat in shape and around seven to eight feet long. The hessian skirt is painted with coloured circles and at the top is a decorated tin face which conceals the dancer's head. Masses of ribbons cover the body of the horse and a long rope tail trails behind. Its stepping, cavorting and shrieking is an exhilarating sight and if you happen to get in the way of its long rope tail as it swings around you won't quickly forget it!

There are currently at least three horses in Minehead: the Traditional Sailors Horse, The Sailors Horse and the Town Horse – sometimes known as the Show Horse. In the past too, it was common for children to appear with their own improvised and rudimentary horses. What appears to be almost an offspring of the Padstow and Minehead 'osses appears at The Hunting of the Earl of Rone at Combe Martin on the North coast of Devon.

## MAYPOLES

There is no real evidence for when the first maypole was erected in the British Isles or why. There are indications of the development of the modern maypole in the 19th century, but a much earlier reference comes from a poem attributed to Chaucer, *Chaunce of the Dice,* where reference is made to the permanent maypole which stood at Cornhill in London by the church of St Andrew Undershaft (so named in fact because of the maypole, which stood by its south door). This was set up by its parishioners every year and was clearly a rallying point. After May Day riots in 1517 it was taken down and some time later, denounced as an idol by a priest, it was burned.

The 16th century sees plenty of references to maypoles; corporations throughout England were paying for maypoles to be painted or decorated with flags and streamers and put up each year. In Exeter in 1588 it is referred to as 'bringing home the summer rod'. Yet, at the end of the 16th and unto the 17th century, we start to find disapproval towards popular revelry and many of the major cities were banning maypoles. Banbury, Bristol, Canterbury, Coventry, Doncaster, Lincoln and London all removed their central poles but there were a few communities that valiantly retained theirs and even made new ones.

The ever-popular notion of the maypole as a phallic symbol is, not surprisingly, post-Freudian, though Thomas Hobbes had previously made the (unfounded) proposition that it was a relic of worship to Priapus, the Roman

18    *An 18th-century illustration of Maypole-raising from Hone's* Every-Day Book

god of male potency.

Maypoles were often built from a single, tall, straight tree, usually pine, larch, elm, birch or ash. The tree would be cut down on May morning, stripped of its branches (except perhaps a few at the top) and carried to the centre of the community with great ceremony. Adorned with flowers and garlands, it would serve as a centrepiece to the May Day celebrations. The ubiquity of Maypoles is demonstrated in the many references to them on pub signs and street names. In some places they are still permanent fixtures; though some are decorated with brightly coloured rings, stripes or spirals, they are adorned only when May Day comes round. Examples include Welford-on-Avon, Warwickshire; Temple Sowerby, Cumbria; Barwick-in-Elmet, West Yorkshire (England's tallest); Ickwell Green in Bedfordshire; Paganhill, Gloucestershire; Belton, near Oakham in Leicestershire and Wellow in Nottinghamshire.

A sense of rivalry between neighbouring villages sometimes led to the theft of maypoles, an activity that almost became a tradition in its own right: modern maypoles are sometimes fitted with burglar alarms.

The 400-year-old May Day event at Ickwell in Bedfordshire centres round a 70-foot red-and-white striped maypole on Ickwell Green. Erected in 1872, this pole is renewed whenever it shows signs of decay, but the ceremony itself is much older; the churchwardens' records of 1561 record payments for spices and fruit for 'bake meats', hops to brew beer, the Morris-dancers' shoes and bells, and the minstrels for the May celebrations. Until the 1920s a Lord and Lady, accompanied by two black-faced 'moggies' along with other supernumeries carying tutti poles would go out overnight with a cart of greenery, and would sing a Night Song while distributing the greenery to households around the village.

In the morning they would return to the houses they had decorated, singing a Day Song to collect ale, food or money. These days the main activity is on the day itself, the celebrations starting with the children's custom of carrying garlands, the election of a May Queen by the village children and her procession, in company with last year's 'monarch', morris dancers, moggies carrying brooms, and characters in attendance, through the village to her coronation; plus the now obligatory ribbon dance round the maypole.

*Villagers carrying the maypole at Barwick-in-Elmet*

## OPPOSITION AND CHANGE

It is true that the Church continually attempted to tame the festivities that they regarded unruly and pagan and the first day of May was, therefore, selected to be the feast of St Philip and St James. Despite this early attempt to displace the older feasts with those of the Church and their saints, May Day continued to flourish and adapt to the pressures. It proved to be one of the most resilient of the festivals. Nevertheless, it was Puritanism which had the greatest effect on the traditional calendar.

The Puritans reacted most strongly to the idolatrous maypole, symbol of pagan worship as they saw it, and Maying and maypole dancing was desribed as 'a heathenish vanity' based on 'superstition and wickedness'.

Somewhat paradoxically, the most vivid descriptions of many of our earlier traditions appear in the Puritans' hysterical outbursts against them. It is the oft-quoted Philip Stubbes who gives us an engaging description of a typical May Day in his 1583 *Anatomie of Abuses*:

> *Against May Day, Whitsunday, or other times, all the young men and maids, old men and wives, run gadding overnight to the woods, groves, hills and mountains, where they spend all the night in pleasant pastimes; and in the morning, they return, bringing with them birch and branches of trees, to deck their assemblies withall.... But the chiefest jewel they bring from thence is their May-pole, which they bring home with great veneration, as thus. They have twenty or forty yoke of oxen, every ox having a sweet nose-gay of flowers placed on the tip of his horns, and these oxen draw home this May-pole (this stinking idol, rather), which is covered all over with flowers and herbs, bound round about with strings, from the top to the bottom, and sometime painted with variable colours, with two or three hundred men, women and children following it with great devotion.*

May Day came under the greatest threat between 1649 and 1660 when England became a republic under the leadership of Oliver Cromwell. King Charles I was publicly beheaded and the monarchy abolished, along with the House of Lords and the Anglican Church. In 1644 the Puritans prohibited all celebrations by Act of Parliament, including Christmas, and the ban lasted until the Restoration of the monarchy under Charles II. It is evident that a large number of customs disappeared during this period but some simply went underground and were rekindled on the return of the King, on May 29th 1660. Some revivals were probably less an indication of the resilience of the custom and more an expression of loyalty to the king, and it is likely that some May Day traditions moved to May 29th for this reason. More movement occurred due to the shift from the Julian to the Gregorian calendar. Britain and Europe used to observe the Julian Calendar, introduced by Julius Caesar and based on an average year of 365 days. As it turned out, this calculation was about 11 minutes too long and by the 16th century astronomers had noted the accumulation of 11 days. In 1582 Pope Gregory XIII introduced the Gregorian Calendar which omitted these 'extra' days. Britain, however, did not begin to observe the Gregorian Calendar until 1752; Chesterfield's Act of March 1751 decreed that in the following year the day after 2nd September would become the 14th. Many people believed they were being cheated and riots broke out in places, with people crying 'Give us back our 11 days!' Even then some people faithfully continued to celebrate their seasonal events based on the old calendar, effectively making their celebrations 11 days late; in fact, by adhering to the old calendar a May event could move to as late as the 9th June.

## OAK APPLE DAY
It was common in some counties of England to have their celebrations on this day, 29th May, rather than the 1st, and even today many people wear oak leaves

in their lapels or hats and decorate their front-door as an annual celebration. At one time, if you didn't do so you risked being 'patched' or pelted with eggs, stung with nettles or kicked and pinched for being a 'Roundhead'. This tradition is still celebrated by children in Sussex as 'Pinch-Bum Day'. King Charles II reputedly hid in the now famous Boscobel oak after the battle of Worcester in 1651, and after the Restoration a variety of ceremonies associated with the oak were introduced on the 29th May. Others include Founders Day at the Chelsea Royal Hospital, London, during which the Chelsea pensioners parade with sprigs of oak leaves on their scarlet jackets. A similar event takes place at Lord Leycester's Hospital in Warwick.

Grovely Rights is another custom that moved to the 29th May, celebrating the rights of the villagers of Wishford Magna in Wiltshire to collect fuel wood from Grovely Forest; a privilege now protected by the Wishford Magna Oak Apple Club. Prior to the Restoration these the rights had to be claimed in front of the high altar in Salisbury Cathedral between Maundy Thursday and Whit Monday, and a formal declaration must still be made there every year for the privilege to continue.

At Castleton in Derbyshire, Oak Apple Day is their famous Garland Day. The garland takes a group of men hours to make, attaching knots of wild flowers and leaves to a hive-shaped frame. Women make a large posy of flowers known as the Queen, which is later inserted in the top of the men's garland. The Garland King and his Lady parade round village and on the second ride the King carries the 60-pound garland. Accompanied by a band and dancers the troupe visit the village pubs for refreshment and the day concludes with lively dancing.

It has generally been accepted that the garland's origins were in some ancient ceremony, and the flower bedecked man consequently lead to an association with the Jack-in-the-Green. Then a 1977 television programme boldly asserted it was actually a remnant of a human sacrifice ritual once performed in the area! This was a litle uncomfortable for some local people but fortunately local records proved that it had in fact evolved from of a rush-bearing ceremony dating from around a hundred years earlier. Bell-ringers had once accompanied a rush cart with a garland, and called at the houses of wealthy towns people for hospitality. Over the century the cart had disappeared and the procession was joined by Morris dancers, who were replaced by local schoolgirls in white by 1897. In 1916 maypole dancing was instituted, a 'king' and 'consort' appeared in historic costume and the event became a folk pageant with a garland committee formed in 1948.

An excuse to move May celebrations to a later date was probably welcome for some people in the north of England. As at Castleton, a number of these events rely heavily on flowering plants and greenery, and the slightly later germination in the north must have made it difficult to gather sufficient blooms. A very bad spell of rain before the ceremony in the early 1980s caused some anxiety about the supply of flowers, and the villagers put out a request on Radio Sheffield for assistance. Fortunately there was a generous response and with that, and 'Interflora', the day went as normal.

Elsewhere in Derbyshire the greenery and flowers may well be carefully cultivated for use in an annual well-dressing ceremony – another custom whose antiquity was believed to go back to pre-Christian times. Water was highly respected as the basis of life and regular ceremonies were held at springs and wells to appease the water deities thought to inhabit them. Despite opposition from the Church and the rededicating of many wells to more 'respectable' Christian saints, these 'holy wells' were still revered and visited for the curative properties of their waters. The ceremonies became a thanksgiving for pure water, but waters were thought more potent if drunk on particular days and

May Day and Ascension Day were regarded as particularly propitious. The ceremonies involve the wells being 'dressed' with large framed panels decorated with elaborate mosaic-like pictures made of flowers and leaves. Large, shallow wooden frames are filled with smooth moist clay onto which are pressed leaves, petals, berries, mosses, pines and other natural materials to make up the colourful image.

The first dressings of the season occur in early May, followed by Tissington in Derbyshire on Ascension Day, with Etwell and Wirksworth — with nine wells — later in the month. Dressings continue throughout the summer in Derbyshire and north Nottinghamshire, with one or two in Staffordshire and at Bisley in Gloucestershire.

There has been a noticeable increase in the number of wells dressed over the past 25 years, with over 160 recorded in 2005.

A garland of a very different kind was paraded by the milkmaids of London and the home counties in the 19th century. Their garland was an arrangement of trays, plates and other silverware. Frequently escorted by musicians, the milkmaids danced through the streets and would call at the houses of their regular customers to collect tips. The origins of the custom lay in the mid-17th century, when the London milkmaids danced with their pails and with their heads crowned with flowers. May Day was also observed by chimney sweeps and they too would parade through the streets, sometimes together with the milk maids.

> *Look the garland dances!*
> *When was such a wonder scene?*
> *Oh, I find as it advances*
> *There's a Jack within the green*

During the following century there are reports of milkmaids accompanied by chimney sweeps (their faces washed, whitened or rouged with 'Dutch pink'), musicians, imps, clowns, a Lord and Lady and finally a Jack-in-the-Green.

Jack-in-the-Green was a curious addition and was a man entirely encased in a pyramidal framework of wood or wicker covered with green leaves. Later, it was he who earned the garland of silver flagons and dishes on his frame. Not surprisingly, regular reports are found of the participants ending their day with 'drunken behaviour and vulgarity' and there are frequent comments of general public disapproval – as well as direct court action. The parade gradually became more subdued, probably partly a result of the 1840 Act of Parliament forbidding the use of the 'climbing boys' who risked life and limb cleaning inside the chimneys.

Reports of the Jack-in-the-Green character continue up to the First World War and, more recently, there have been a number of revivals – very often by Morris sides. He can be seen in the May Day celebrations at Hastings in Sussex, Rochester and Whitstaple in Kent. This Jack-in-the-Green, however, is frequently erroneously referred to as a 'Green Man' and there are a number of revived May customs featuring this character. The Green Man was a term first used in 1939 by Lady Raglan, a member of the Folklore Society, to describe the foliated head found on bosses and carvings in many medieval churches – a man's head intertwined with twigs or leaves which often sprouted from mouth and nostrils. Raglan was clearly influenced by ideas of pre-Christian spirits of nature and fertility; thus Jack of the milkmaids became associated with the veneration of primeval deities.The carvings in question, however, all date from the 14th to 16th centuries.

To confuse matters even more, a Jack o' the Green character is mentioned during the 19th century, simply described as carrying a walking stick and floral

*Jack-in-the-Green, Oxford, photographed by Henry Taunt in 1886*

wreath. A character regularly associated with the May Day celebrations, however, is Robin Hood, and both these characters are commonly confused with the Jack-in-the-Green. Robin Hood was a prominent character in early May games and has been incorporated into the May Day repertoire, where he became interchangeable with the Lord or King of the May as well as Jack-in-the-Green. It was the Victorians who finally shaped the image of Robin Hood as the English folk hero we think of today.

## ASCENSION DAY

By the 4th century the Church was commemorating Pentecost and by the next century had fixed the date on the 7th Sunday after Easter, with the 6th Thursday marking the ascension of Christ into heaven. Early records show that church bells were rung on Ascension Day and the paschal candle, which had burned since Easter week, would be lit for the last time and removed as a sign that Christ had risen. Churches were also decorated with garlands, but only in London.

Holy-well water was used for curative and divination purposes on Ascension Day. Rain falling on this day was considered to be holy water direct from heaven; a teaspoonful added to the dough while making bread was guaranteed to keep it light. Many weather traditions are associated with Ascension Day, and in Staffordshire a piece of hawthorn gathered on Ascension Day would be hung in the rafters each year to protect the house against lightning. In Nottinghamshire, it was believed that an egg laid on Ascension Day and placed in the roof of a house would protect against fire and other calamities.

When life was still tied to the agricultural year, it was common in most places to process around the fields, often on the three days before the feast of the Ascension, in order to bless the growing crops. These processions were known as Rogations, from the Latin rogare, 'to ask'. It is Ascension Day, or Rogation Day, that we now know as the day for Beating the Bounds or Boundaries of the parish. In some places they were known as Cross days, from a time when processions were headed by priests with crosses; whilst other localities called them 'Gang Days' derived from the word going. There has been a recent revival of interest in this ceremony which, at one time, had the dual purpose of blessing the land and also keeping up the memory of the parish boundaries in the days before formal maps. Although some are kept up annually, most 'beatings' are done every three or seven years.

These events were nothing if not boisterous. In 19th-century Exeter, the Mayor and Chamber beat the city boundaries on the Tuesday before Ascension Day accompanied by the 'Blue Boys' of St John's Hospital who carryied poles bedecked with flowers. The company skirted the quay by boat, but were drenched with water when passing the ships; on other parts of the route the boat was upset or some of the party immersed in the water. Apparently it was considered lawful on Ascension Day to throw water over passers-by and in many streets passers-by who did not donate money were splashed with water, a custom known as 'stratting'.

In York, the parish clerk of All Saints was struck on the back of his legs with bundles of sage by the local lads while marking the boundary stones and it is quite traditional to bump any child on the boundary marker in order that the locations would be 'sorely remembered'. In London, a schoolboy is held upside-down by his feet from a boat in the Thames where there runs a boundary line. After a luckless 'upset' in the early 1980s, the elected pupil is now always checked to have emptied his coat pockets first!

But not only children are subjected to such indignities. On the Wednesday nearest 18th May at Newbiggin-by-the Sea in Northumberland, the freeholders hold an annual meeting. They check the moor and the boundaries and any new householders have to undergo an initiation ceremony at the 'dunting stone'. The newcomer is hoisted by the bailiff and others and is 'dunted' three times on the stone. Until the 1920s the route was ridden and accompanied by a piper, but these days it is travelled on foot though new householders are still bumped three times. At one time these freeholders would have all been fishermen. Newbiggin Moor is divided into a number of 'stints', or plots, and each freeholder owns at least one stint; today a golf club pays for one section. Any householder whose property backs on to the moor pays around twenty pence a year in exchange for some nuts – which are given out during a ceremony dating back to a 13th-century charter from King John.

The most arduous boundary tour is certainly that at Chudleigh, Devon, which occurs every seven years. Not only is it 21 miles long but a volunteer has to swim the River Teign at one point while the others in the procession take a detour by road. Additionally, a bus is nowadays required for the whole company to cross a dual-carriageway which has been built in recent times. Other ancient boundaries have long since been built over, but the ceremonies continue; in Oxford the bounds are beaten in Marks & Spencer, university buildings, the covered market and a pub, among other establishments.

Another movable feast day was Whitsun and its spelling – Hwit, Wit or Whit – has changed over the centuries too. The word is usually accepted to mean 'white' and a reference to the garments used by baptised converts on Whit Sunday, though another association is with a tradition of the rich giving all their cow's milk to the poor. White became shortened to 'Whit', as in Whitby, and others turned it into 'Witsondai' – the day when the Apostles received their 'wit' or knowledge and the gift of tongues from the Holy Ghost

After the Whitsunday evening service in St Briavels parish church in the Forest of Dean, the annual dole of bread and cheese is distributed from a wall nearby. Distribution is rather a mute word, for the bread and cheeses have been cut into very small cubes and are thrown into or at the crowd of expectant recipients, by two locals standing on the wall. Each shower of food precipitates scrambling or elbowing by men, women and children attempting to catch some. Hats held out, skirts lifted up at the hem and even upturned umbrellas are brought into play in an attempt catch the morsels. In earlier times it is known that miners and quarry-men would often wear a pouch to work containing the year's bread and cheese portions as lucky charms. More recently participants are seen to casually throw down the bread and cheese that they had saved from the previous year as the first shower is thrown.

On Coopers Hill, Brockworth, near Birdlip in Gloucestershire, cheese features in a preposterous event, formerly held on Whit Monday but now transferred to the Spring Bank Holiday Monday. Not for the faint-hearted, the 'sport' involves
**30** chasing large, round Gloucester cheeses down a 250-yard, 1-in-3 slope.

After the master of ceremonies, who wears a white coat, ribbons and a top hat, has announced the beginning of the game, the cheeses are rolled separately down the slope followed by young men in hot pursuit. (There are races for women too.) The winner is the person who reaches the bottom first. As the cheese reaches speeds of 70 miles per hour, any hope of catching it is misplaced to say the least. There are frequent injuries, to spectators as well as participants – to be hit by a flying 8-pound Double Gloucester, or even a stray runner, is no laughing matter. In 1982, eight spectators were injured, not by the cheese, however, but by a freak lightning bolt which hit the tree they were sheltering under.

Why do they do it? Perhaps it is sufficient to see it as a rite of passage for the men of Brockworth or, not unlike the St Briavels Dole, the Cooper's Hill Cheese Rolling may have evolved from a medieval way of protecting locals' rights to common land and to maintain grazing rights for the villagers of Brockworth.

In earlier times the Cooper Hill festivities included numerous other activities: wrestling matches, gurning, sack races, and a fair at the top of the hill where a maypole still stands. 'After the wake was over, ruffianism commenced', a local recalled in the late 1890s. 'The village feuds, grudges and personal quarrels were then settled. Sanguinary and prolonged fights followed'.

*A winning cheese-roller at Cooper's Hill, Birdlip, Gloucestershire*

Whitsun was also the time for walks, processions and feasts associated with local clubs, particularly Village Friendly Societies – an early form of insurance society. There would be parades around the whole of the community with members in their best clothes, carrying staves and banners and often accompanied by a local or club band. Large numbers centred on Manchester and Salford and across the Pennines in Yorkshire. Frequently, it would also be celebrated with a fair and the day might end with a club dinner or a feast, often provided by club funds. As the Societies were teetotal, it is probable that these events were deliberately promoted to rival the Whitsun Ale festivities. The North of England Galas, with their processions and banners, built on these traditions.

## STICKS AND BELLS...MORRIS DANCERS

*'First of all the wild heads of the parish conventing together, chose themselves a grand captain (of mischief) whom they enoble with the title of my Lord of Misrule, and him they crown with great solemnity, and adopt for their king. The king anointed, chooseth for the twenty, forty, three score or a hundred lusty guts like unto himself, to wait upon His Lordly Majesty, and to guard his noble person. Then every one of these his men he investeth with his liveries of green, yellow or some other light wanton colour. And as though that were not bawdy enough I should say, they bedeck themselves with gold rings, precious stones and other jewels: This done, they tie about either leg twenty or forty bells with rich handkerchieves in their hands, and sometimes laid across over their shoulders and necks, borrowed for the most part of their pretty Mopsies and loving Bessies, for bussying them in the dark. These things set in order, they have their hobby horses, dragons and other antiques, together with their bawdy pipes and thundering drummers, to strike up the Devil's Dance withall, then march these heathen company towards the church and churchyard, their pipers piping, drummers thundering, their stumps dancing, their bells jingling, their handkerchieves swinging about their heads like madmen, their hobby horses and other monsters skirmishing amongst the throng: and in this sort they go to the church ...'*

John Stubbes' description of 16th-century Morris dancers is wonderfully evocative. Morris dancing was traditionally associated with Whit week, though nowadays, of course, it is seen at other times of the year. But what does it all mean? There are whispers of ritual origins – pagan sacrificial rites, fertility cults, scaring evil spirits, even controlling the weather. Whether these were once ritual dances or not has to remain a mystery – we simply don't know.

Certainly central to many village celebrations, they are known to have been popular in the royal courts and guilds from the 15th century onwards. In fact, the earliest documentary evidence of the Morris dance stems largely from churchwarden's accounts from the 15th century. Early reactions to the traditions, as Stubbes has shown, were not always favourable. The first known eye-witness account of Morris dancing comes from household accounts in 1467 from Laherne, North Cornwall, which mention 'moruske' dancing. Later that century there were further sightings in London and Plymouth. By the age of Elizabeth I it was already the favourite festival dance of the English people and, even then, was regarded as ancient.

The popularity of Morris in the last century was, of course, due to the efforts of Cecil Sharp, who first encountered the dances of the Headington Quarry Morris when he was staying at Headington near Oxford on Boxing Day 1899. He began to collect the dances some time later and published hundreds of examples. The form varies from region to region and these days we can see a fantastic assortment of Morris styles performed throughout the year and throughout the country, including Cotswold Morris dancers with their white costumes, bells and dancing with sticks and hankies; Border Morris and Molly-dancers with their brightly coloured costumes and black faces; not to mention the North West Clog dancers, long sword, North East rapper, garland and stave dancing.

## In conclusion

It is satisfying to think that May Day, among other seasonal events, is still celebrated in many parts of Britain, having survived opposition of many kinds throughout the centuries (and we may feel optimisitc that it will survive the omnipresent requirements of Health and Safety, which are increasingly interfering with longstanding methods of performance and well-tried techniques). It is also gratifying that in Britain today, with its cultural plurality and growing diversity, it is possible to see many recently evolved or imported traditions.

This book is a celebration of the month of May – a glorious month so full of events that regretfully it has been necessary to give just a fleeting glance to many activities that are as prominent, dramatic and colourful as those given a longer mention.

Although we generally respect and marvel at the dances and rituals we may see overseas, it is sad to realise that we know little of our own. Moreover, it seems extraordinary to me that often we are embarrassed by, or even ridicule, our own indigenous cultural traditions. In this book I wanted to celebrate the diversity, vitality and richness of the organic, living vernacular arts still found in the contemporary folk culture of our own islands.

So whether you welcome the summer by taking part in a communal tradition that has developed and evolved through the centuries, or indulge in a Victorian evocation of an ancient seasonal revelry, or get together with you community, family and friends to participate in a recently constructed or revived occasion, you will be taking part in a celebration of 'people celebrating themselves' – essential and elemental for a healthy society.

OPPOSITE *Shropshire Bedlams*

# MAY GARLANDS

May Dolling garlands varied in from simple posies or flower chains wreathed around staves to elaborate double or treble hoops covered with flowers, or even tall pyramids of greenery. In 18th-century Lincolnshire, willow wands were covered in cowslips and known as 'May Gads'. In Northumberland children would carry cushions of greenery with flowers peeping through.

A splendid description from the 1880s comes from Flora Thompson from Juniper Hill on the Oxfordshire–Northamptonshire border:

> It consisted of a bell-shaped wooden frame four feet tall, covered in primroses, violets, cowslips, wallflowers, oxlips, and currant flowers. A knot of especially fine blooms was placed on top and a china doll, termed 'the lady', hung in the centre. White muslin was draped over it and it was hoisted on a broomstick. Made in the schoolroom, it was collected at six o'clock on May Morning by all the parish children aged seven to eleven; the girls in white or light frocks and the boys in bright ribbon knots and bows and sashes worn crosswise. They formed a procession led by a boy with a flag and a girl carrying a money-box. Then came the garland, between two bearers, and a May Queen and King, the former crowned with daisies and wearing a white veil and gloves. The royal couple were followed by two maids of honour, a lord and lady with maids of their own, a footman and his lady, and then the remaining children.

TOP *Children with garland, photographed by Henry Taunt*

BOTTOM *Bampton-in-the-Bush garlands, Oxfordshire*

# PADSTOW 'OBBY 'OSS DAY

Padstow, Cornwall. The 'Old 'Oss' and 'Blue Ribbon 'Oss' each conceal a man under an enormous frame draped with heavy, black tarpaulin and many layers of black paint. His head is covered with a heavy mask representing the rider. A symbolic horse-head and real horse-hair tail is fixed to the rim of the frame. To the accompaniment of accordions and singing the 'Oss is teased and danced through the streets of Padstow all day long.

Occasionally the tune changes pace almost to a dirge and the 'Oss sinks to the ground; the teazer then caresses the 'Oss with his club and to a cry of 'Oss, Oss' and renewed beating of the drums, it springs back to life.

It is said that when licentiousness developed around the cavortings of the original 'Old 'Oss' in the 19th century, some of the more sober members of the community constructed their own – the Blue Ribbon 'Oss – taking its name from the Blue Ribbon of the temperance movement. After the First World War it was renamed the Armistice, or Peace 'Oss, but, obviously, this ideal was shattered in 1939 and the original name was reinstated.

The relentless and hypnotic beat of the drums, the sound of soaring voices of the Mayers singing their annual May song … the words, the passion and emotion is absorbed by the crowd almost to synchronise the collective pulse and heart-beat. Old and young, frail and active all share the same intensity of spirit. Unquestionably the most important event of the year, emotion runs high on Mayday: with tears of joy and affection, of grief and loss and a true contemplation of the preceding year and beyond. It is not difficult to sense that the 'Oss and Mayday symbolises more… it's a united proclamation –

*Old 'Oss, Padstow*

almost 'a clenched fist' in the face of the ravages of time and outside influences. The 'Oss can be seen as a communal pace-maker and, on Mayday, it recharges the community and the good fellowship of the people of Padstow.

One of the earliest descriptions of the Padstow celebrations comes from the diary of one Paul Robins, who was sailing for Quebec in 1846:

> *May 1st. This most disgusting scene was acted by the sailors. An ugly mask was worn by one of them, who went astride a pole shaped in the end to be a very bad imitation of a horse's head with a tail behind. A man thus masked, and covered with tarred canvas down to the feet, gallopped about the decks after the sailors and passengers and, then having greased and smutted their hands, they rubbed them over the faces of each other and the passengers whom they could catch. Most of us kept below, but Dr Hooper being cook got a black face, and would have fared worse had he not held up the poker in self defence; and John Healand and Sampson shared the same fate.*

RIGHT  *Blue Ribbon 'Oss, Padstow May Day*

OVER  *Old 'Oss, Padstow May Day*

# MINEHEAD
# HOBBY HORSE

The Minehead horse appears initially on 30 April, 'Warning Eve', then at 6.00 am on the first of May the horse bows three times to the sun to greet the day. It then processes into Minehead accompanied by 'sailors', playing drums and melodeons. It gambols around the town and spends the next three evenings performing around Minehead and soliciting money from those it meets. The horse is anarchic – it chases visitors and stops cars and motorcyclists without trepidation. On the last evening, at a place known as Cher, the 'booty ceremony' takes place. A 'victim' is seized from the crowd, held horizontally by legs and arms, and the 'prow' of the horse bows down ten times over them accompanied by the crowd's call of 'Ah one, Ah two, Ah three ….', after which the victim dances hand in hand with the horse.

The ceremony at one time was a much rougher affair with a pair of wooden pincers used to catch victims – especially those who refused to pay. Characters known as 'gullivers', beribboned in a similar way to the horse, would threaten passers-by. Once, this got out of hand and a gentleman was fatally wounded, so the gullivers and pincers were abandoned, though gullivers have reappeared in more recent times, however, with the Town Horse which is stabled at Alcombe.

*Minehead Hobby Horse*

# HUNTING THE EARL OF RONE

The Hunting of the Earl of Rone takes place on the late Spring Bank Holiday weekend. The horse here is a mass of colourful ribbons and is accompanied by a fool, dressed in a smock and tatters and carrying a besom broom, and a troop of scarlet-coated grenadiers carrying muskets. They process through the village with musicians and villagers in 19th-century dress, led by a line of women carrying a rope-barrier decorated with flowers. On Sunday the procession travels from the shore-end of the village to The Top George public house. On Monday the route is reversed and events reach their conclusion. The central masked figure, the Earl of Rone, is captured by the grenadiers. The Earl is dressed in a padded, hessian suit with a string of hard sea-biscuits round his neck and sits astride a real donkey adorned with flowers and a matching sea-biscuit collar. Seated back-to-front on the donkey, the Earl is regularly 'shot' by the Grenadiers, usually outside the various public houses along the route, but is revived by the attentions of the hobby horse and fool. By sunset, they have found their way to the beach; here a huge circle is formed and everyone dances with the horse. The Earl is brought into this circle and the captain of grenadiers orders the final execution, after which the Earl is thrown into the sea.

The original revels were banned in 1837 after a local man died after falling from a wall – presumably due to certain excesses – but the event was 'reconstructed' in 1978 and you would now never know it had stopped. It is based on the legend that the Elizabethan rebel, the Earl of Tyrone, was wrecked on the North Devon coast during his escape from Ireland. Surviving on ship's biscuits, he was finally captured by militia in the local woods, taken to Exeter and executed. The fact that there is no historical truth in this legend does nothing to dampen the spirit of the day.

ABOVE  *Hobby Horse and Fool*

OVER  *Grenadiers capture the Earl of Rone*

47

# HASTINGS JACK-IN-THE-GREEN

Mad Jack's Morris, in Hastings, celebrate May Day by dancing the sun up at dawn. At the May Bank Holiday they also support the first appearance of Jack-in-the-Green, a man completely covered in a wicker framework around ten feet tall, covered in fresh greenery and topped with a floral crown and ribbons. To 'awake the spirit of summer', he parades throughout the day accompanied by masses of Morris, clog and sword dancers – even giants and animals – from other parts of the country.

This is really an exciting and colourful spectacle, with Jack and friends processing around the old and new parts of the town before climbing up to Hastings Castle. Here, after performances by the visiting teams, he is symbolically slain by cutting off his crown. Pieces of the Jack are distributed to the crowds. Similar characters appear at Rochester and Whitstable in Kent, also accompanied by a multitude of Morris sides, and spectators are desperate to take a piece of greenery from the 'departed' Jack for good luck.

*Hastings, Jack-in-the-Green followers*

# HELSTON FLORAL DANCE

May 8th is the Feast of the Apparition of St Michael, the patron saint of Helston, and the local event became famous through its 'Floral Dance' tune. This was only introduced into the proceedings in the 1920s, however, while the 'Furry Day' was well established as a festival in 1600; its name reflects the Old English 'fery', Cornish 'feur' and Latin 'feria', meaning feast or holy day.

These days the streets are decorated with greenery and flowers, there is a Mayer's carol 'The Hal-and Tow' which is sung in the morning with a play and, of course, the famous Floral Dance. Though this may not be the oldest dance in the British Isles, as some would like to believe, it is certainly one the last remaining of the processional dances which were at one time common throughout Cornwall. During the day characters bearing greenery accompany various historical personalities: St George, Robin Hood and Aunt Mary Moses join St Michael and a Dragon. All the dances are led by Helston Town Band and the climax of the morning is over 150 couples in formal dress begin the principal dance as the Guildhall clock strikes twelve. The dancers literally weave their way through the whole town – right through houses and shops – bringing good luck to each residence and symbolically bonding the whole neighbourhood. Everyone joins can join in the final dance at 5pm is one for everyone to join and dress can be informal.

*Children's Dance at the beginning of the day*

May 8th is Helstons 'Furry Day', made famous by its 'Floral Dance' tune. A wonderful account occurs in the Gentleman's Magazine for 1790:

*Very early in the morning some troublesome rogues go round the streets with drums disturbing their neighbours and singing. The people make it a general holiday, and anyone found working is carried on a pole to a wide part of the river where he must attempt to leap across it or pay a fine. About 9.00 am they (the people, including the rogues) appear before the school and demand a holiday for the Latin boys, which is always granted. They then go and collect money from house to house. About noon they assemble and dance hand in hand round the streets accompanied by a fiddler, and this continues until it is dark. This is a 'Faddy'. In the afternoon the local gentry go to some farm houses and have tea, syllabub, and other refreshment, and then return in a Morris-dance to the town, and dance through the streets until it is dark, claiming the right to go through any person's house, in one door and out at another. Here it used to end, but a corruption has now crept in, for the gentlemen now conduct their partners, elegantly dressed in white muslin, to the ballroom of the Archangel where they finish their dance, and after supper faddy it to their respective homes.*

*Helston Furry Dancers promenading through shops*

# BARWICK-IN-ELMET MAYPOLE

England's tallest maypole stands at Barwick-in-Elmet, near Leeds; replaced in May 2005 it currently stands at 88 feet 6 inches tall. It is taken down every three years on Easter Monday to be redecorated  and raised on the late May Bank Holiday; its elaborate garlands are traditionally set in place about 50 feet up and, at the end of the ceremony, a climber shins up the pole and spins the fox-shaped weather vane at the very top; his reward, a single bell from a garland as a keepsake. It was an astounding event, involving ropes and pulleys and a series of ladders of increasing height. In 2005 it was still astounding, though as much for the requirement of hard hats and use of JCB equipment to satisfy Health and Safety requirements. More than one observer on that day felt that the proximity of the industrial machinery to the crowds posed a greater threat of injury than the older, tried and tested methods. The teams of villagers were still there to pull ropes to guide the pole into place and to raise the four bell-shaped garlands, constructed by villagers from hundreds of hand-sewn rosettes and dozens of bells hanging from ribbons.

*Climbing the maypole at Barwick*

# ABBOTSBURY GARLANDS

On 13th May, children carry two elaborate garlands of flowers around the quiet village of Abbotsbury in Dorset. They call at each household, requesting gifts of money from householders. The flower garlands are attached to shaped frames, one is decorated with wild flowers and the other with cultivated garden blooms. The money collected is shared out equally among the children later in the day. In the evening a third garland is constructed by the parents, from left-over stems of both garden and wild flowers. This is then taken round the village by the older schoolchildren (who are unable to get the day off) and is usually laid at the foot of the war memorial at the end of the day. This tradition was interrupted in 1954 when an over-zealous policeman, a newcomer in the district, stopped the children and confiscated their money for breaking the begging laws. The following day, however, an even bigger procession of older villagers complained to the Chief Constable about this attempt to destroy their age-old tradition.

In former times Garland Day marked the beginning of the fishing season and each boat had its own garland which, having been blessed, was taken in procession to the shore, put on the bow of the boat and taken out to sea. Each garland was cast into the waves as a safeguard for the lives of the fishermen.

*Abbotsbury garland, 1979*

# GROVELY FOREST RIGHTS

The villagers of Wishford Magna in Wiltshire's Wylye valley have an ancient common right to collect loose wood or broken branches from the nearby forest of Grovely to use as fuel. Court proceedings from 1603 set out the complete rights of villagers, privileges that existed 'by ancient custom and time out of mind' and included 'grazing all manner of beasts and cattle' as well as the removal of boughs on Whit Monday. Although these rights were regularly taken up, the was instituted in 1892 to safeguard them. The right to take away as much dead wood as can be carried personally still applies and is verified in the Commons Registration Act of 1965.

The modern day starts with a boisterous tin can band in the early hours and villagers go out in the night 'maying' to cut green boughs which they carry back to the village and later parade. One large 'marriage bough' is hoisted to the top of the church tower thought to bring luck to couples that are to be married in the year. Houses in the village are decorated with greenery and prizes are later given for the best dressed as well as for the largest boughs gathered from the Forest.

*Early morning gathering of boughs for the church tower*

Most important is the morning visit to Salisbury Cathedral, six miles away. Here the company, headed by women bearing faggots or sprigs of oak which are given to the Dean, go up to the high altar and declare loudly, 'Grovely!, Grovely!, Grovely! and all Grovely!' This and the reading of the charter reaffirms their rights to gather the wood for another year. A dance is performed inside the Cathedral as well as outside on the green by women holding sprigs of oak on their heads. The same women, now carrying bundles of dry firewood on their heads, lead the impressive procession through Wishford village and celebrate another year under the wonderful Oak Apple Club's banner.at the head of the procession bearing the club's motto: 'Grovely! Grovely! Grovely! and all Grovely! Unity is strength.'

# CASTLETON GARLAND DAY

Dressed in Stuart period costumes, the Garland King and his Lady make their appearance in the early evening on 29th May. On white horses, they parade around the village the 'lady' riding side-saddle. After their first ride, the King has the hollow, flower-covered 'garland' placed over his head and shoulders. Over three feet high and weighing about 60 pounds, this garland covers him down to his waist. It is then topped with the 'Queen' and the Garland King has to wear this in procession through the village.

Accompanied by a silver band playing the Garland Tune, a troop of girl dancers dressed in white and carrying posies, and an escort of cubs and brownies, the procession stops at each of the six village pubs for refreshment while the young children dance the 'Garland Dance'. Later they do a ribbon dance around the maypole in the square. When all the pubs have been visited, the King and his consort ride into the churchyard, where the 'Queen' is removed; the main garland is lifted from the King's shoulders and hoisted to the top of the church tower where it is fixed to one of the pinnacles. The 'Queen' posy is later placed on the war memorial by the King and the Last Post is sounded. The end of the day often sees visitors and villagers alike dancing a spirited impromptu dance through the streets.

RIGHT *The Garland King*

OVER *Maypole dancing at Castleton*

# DERBYSHIRE WELL DRESSING

Well-dressing designs are first drawn onto large sheets of paper and then the lines are pricked through to the clay surface using a sharp object. These outlines are usually then emphasised with berries and seeds, the main areas filled in last of all with the colourful petals, usually the day before the dressing ceremony. The completed dressings, which are often 10–12 ft high, will remain bright for about a week depending on the weather. A light spraying with water helps to keep the clay moist and the vegetation fresh. Lichen and oatmeal are regularly used too and even grains of rice and sago. The rule seems to be only organic matter. Spaghetti and even human hair, has been included in more recent dressings and this has led to some controversy. The artistic rivalry between villages is not inconsiderable.

The subjects differ every year and are usually Biblical scenes, though more recently modem themes have been introduced alongside them. Paddington Bear appeared in the Year of the Child and Morris Men in Heritage Year. Whales, dolphins and global warming have been themes in more ecologically aware times. In 1979 the artist John Piper, well known for his stained-glass work in Coventry cathedral, was invited to design a well at Tideswell. He chose the a water deity as his theme but sadly there was a reaction against this by some locals who felt the image was pagan and inappropriate for a holy well. The well was neglected almost immediately, and without a spraying with water it faded very quickly.

ABOVE *Well dressing, Derbyshire.*

RIGHT *Well dressing at Tideswell*

69

# WHITBY PENNY HEDGE

On Ascension Eve, the foreshore on the east side of Whitby harbour sees this most discreet and gentle of ceremonies. The custom probably dates back to Saxon times, though is said to be explained by a 12th-century legend, which tells that in October 1159, William de Bruce, Ralph de Percy and Allatson were hunting a wild boar at Eskdaleside. The boar ran into a hermitage and in the quarrel that ensued the hermit was fatally wounded. The Abbot's court brought the men to trial for manslaughter and hunting in the Abbot's chase. Found guilty, a penance was laid upon them: that they and their descendants would assemble at sunrise every Ascension Eve and cut stout stakes and yedders, traditionally 'by means of a knife worth not more than a penny', to build a horngarth or hedge on the shore. The ceremony still ends with a horn being blown and a cry of 'Out on ye; Out on Ye; Out on Ye for the heinous crime'.

The hedge is built in the presence of the bailiff and steward of the manor, and by tradition has to withstand three tides or the builders will forfeit their lands. Often the hedge from the previous year has to be taken down in order to build the new one, so effective is its construction. Indeed, the hedge has never fallen and continues to be built to resist the strongest tide.

*Whitby Penny Hedge*

# BEATING THE BOUNDS,
# TOWER OF LONDON

The beating of the bounds of the Tower Liberty, adjoining the Tower of London, takes place every three years. After a private service at the Chapel Royal of St Peter and Vincula a large procession comprising chief warder, chaplain, chapel choir, royalty and children dwelling in the Tower, yeomen warders and many other dignitaries, visit each of the 31 boundary stones. At each the chief warder raises his mace and the procession stops. After the chaplain's shout of 'Cursed is he who moves his neighbour's landmark' the chief warder instructs the choir to 'Whack it, boys, whack it!' with willow canes, which they do with alarming enthusiasm until told to stop.

The nearby parish of All Hallows by the Tower has an annual perambulation, part of the boundary is on the Thames itself. It also coincides with part of the Tower Liberty grounds, and every third year there is a confrontation between the two. There is a record of one of their beaters dying after an incident with their rivals in the 16th century and there is always an edge to the booing that ensues.

# BEATING THE BOUNDS,
# ST MICHAELS, OXFORD

At the parish church of Oxford, St Michael's at the North Gate, the annual ceremony goes back to 1428. After morning communion and prayers the priest, choir-master, choir boys and parishioners are each given a cane for the beating. Until the late 19th century all the city boundaries were beaten, a feat that apparently took 13 hours; it is deemed sufficient now just to do the Parish stones, but there are 22 of them. Each stone is marked in chalk with a cross, and in each corner the letters S M N G (representing St Michaels at the North Gate) together with the current year. These markings can be seen throughout the year all over Oxford. The priest calls out 'Mark, Mark, Mark!' and the beaters shout the same as they beat the stones.

Every year shoppers at Oxford's Marks & Spencer are surprised by the troop of choristers, academics and visitors who enter the lingerie department and proceed yell 'Mark...' and beat a spot on the carpet with their long canes. The store was built directly over the parish boundary, as were various university buildings, the covered market, the Town Hall, Boots the Chemists, a bike shop, a garage and the Roebuck Inn. Libation is provided at a number of these stops and the day finishes with lunch at Lincoln College with an optional ivy beer — a special brew containing aromatic ground ivy; one is wise to follow the advice given and only drink one pint. This diversion is followed by a scramble by the children (wearing gloves) for hot pennies thrown from the college roof.

*Beating the Bounds in Oxford's Marks & Spencer*

# BREAD AND CHEESE
# DOLE, ST BRIAVELS

The earliest record of the bread and cheese dole at St Briavels, in the Forest of Dean, Gloucestershire, dates from 1779, when the distribution was made inside the church from the galley into the congregation. It seems the 'portions' were then larger, but just as stale, and were used as pellets, with the parson getting 'his share' according to 19th-century records. It was transferred mid-century to the church tower, later to the church wall and, nowadays, the nearby wall.

There is a folk story that tells of the local Earl of Hereford withdrawing the villagers' right to collect fuel-wood from the forest. When his wife implored him to reconsider, the Earl agreed on condition that she rode Godiva-like around the area. This she accepted and rode naked around the forest known as the Hudnalls. So villagers may still gather wood and, in recognition of her consideration, the early vil-lagers established a fund for the poor; a charity that was subsequently replaced by the bread and cheese dole.

*Reaching up for bread and cheese at St Briavels*

# COOPER'S HILL
# CHEESE ROLLING

This remarkable event is known as Cheese Rolling. It is sheer lunacy – the maddest and most dangerous ceremony in the May calendar, possibly even the annual one. Each competitor is marked with chalk to prevent cheat-ing then lines up at the top of the hill. The master of ceremonies wearing a white smock and top-hat with ribbons, commences each race with: 'One to be ready, Two to be steady, Three to prepare, Four to be off'. The cheese is released, usually by a local dignitary, on the shout of 'three', and on 'four' the contestants hurl themselves after it. Runners catapult into space: they collide into, bounce off, fall over and overtake each other during their bone-cracking descent. Any attempt to run is short-lived and, at the bottom, participants are caught or tackled by members of the local Rugby team in an effort to break their fall. When the race is over (usually after around 10 or 12 seconds) the St John's ambulance crew gather up the bodies and tend to their injuries. Sometimes the paramedics have to resort to rescue equipment, even abseiling from the top to reach victims, who are then strapped to a stretcher and lowered to the bottom.

RIGHT  *Cooper's Hill cheese rolling: the start*

OVER  *Risking life and limb*

# COTSWOLD OLYMPICS

The Friday following the late Spring Bank Holiday sees the Cotswold Olympic Games at Dover's Hill, Chipping Camden. Formerly held on the Friday after Whitsun, it is at least 500 years old, 'instituted in the reign of James I by Robert Dover, an attorney'. Featuring football, skittles, quoits, shovel board, cudgel, cock fighting, bowling, wrestling, pitching the bar, horse racing, ringing of bells, jumping in sacks … and (even today) the ancient but painful sport of 'shin kicking'. The games start at 7.30 pm with the firing of a gun from a wooden castle. The day ends with a torchlit procession by spectators from Dovers' Hill, high above Chipping Camden, down into the town itself, where the entertainment continues.

Events recommence the following day with the Scuttlebrook Wake, is a glorious May festival named after the brook that runs through the town. It starts at 2.30 pm with the local Morris side pulling a carriage bearing the May Queen elect and her entourage. In the town square the previous Queen crowns the new and the usual May activities follow.

In 1894, Robert Blatchford's *Merrie England* was published. With its enthusiasm for, and a propositionto return to, a basic rural life associated with a revival of handicrafts, it was clearly significant in its influence. It certainly encouraged the London-based Guild of Handicraft and the Peasant Arts Fellowship, who were keen to combine their ideals of 'socialist utopia' with the 'festivals of rural England'. The Guild eventually moved to the Cotswold town of Chipping Campden in 1902, and within no time was promoting 'ancient' May games, Morris dancing, Revels and May Queens.

*Chipping Campden May celebrations photographed by Henry Taunt in 1897*

# CORBY POLE FAIR

Corby, Northamptonshire, one time synonymous with steel production, has an older part of town which is the scene of a remarkable fair. The old village is transformed into a colourful spectacle, with a pageant, floats, an ox roast, bonfire, fair, celebration dances, games and displays not to mention the old favourites climbing the greasy pole and tug-of-war – but only every 20 years!

The next is due in 2022, and magnificent and elaborate archways of garlanded flowers are built on the entrance roads to the Fair in the Old Town. Thus barricaded and manned, no-one passes without paying a toll. Any man refusing to do so is hoisted onto a pole and taken – rather painfully – to one of three sets of stocks. Women are taken more decorously in a chair, but all are locked up until someone pays.

Although Henry III established the right to hold two annual fairs in 1226 and Queen Elizabeth I granted a Royal charter in 1585, giving local people exemption from certain tolls and dues, the first documented celebration of this 'ancient' Pole Fair is only 1862.

It is the Royal charter that is read at the specially placed toll-gate entrances to the village, just after villagers have been awakened by the old parish church bells at dawn. A short service of blessing is given and the Fair is then officially opened with the local rector, the chairman of the council and the oldest person born in the village all being carried shoulder-high on chairs. They have the 'honour', however, of being the first occupants of the stocks.

# BAMPTON MORRIS

Records show that Morris dancing played a central role in many of the spring and summer village festivities. Obviously it was banned by Puritans but, unlike other activities, it did not really regain its popularity until the 20th century. Frequently, as men transferred to industrial work from their countryside activities, the Morris began to decline but in certain villages the dancing has always been supported. By tradition, the first appearance of the season would have been Whit Monday but many have shifted to the Spring Bank Holiday. Bampton Morris, from Bampton-in-the Bush in Oxfordshire, is one of the few Cotswold or South Midlands sides that have performed relatively continuously. Others in the region are the neighbouring teams of Abingdon, Headington Quarry and Chipping Camden.

Bampton Traditional Morris men dance with handkerchiefs. Typical of a Cotswold side, they wear white clothing and ribboned arm-bands with bells attached to pads tied below the knees. They also wear bowlers with flowers around them. They are accompanied by musicians on a melodeon or fiddle, a fool who dances with the team and interacts with spectators and another who carries a fruit cake impaled on a flower bedecked sword. He dispenses portions of the cake to those who care to donate a few pence for the dancers.

RIGHT AND OVER  *Bampton Traditional Morris dancers*

# CALENDAR OF MAY EVENTS

The following is by no means a definitive list, but presents a selection of the May Day events that can be visited around the country. Please respect the event and those taking part, and enjoy!

**1st May**
OXFORD
May Morning-Magdalen Tower at 6.00 am followed by Morris dancing in the streets

SOUTHAMPTON, Hampshire
Singing on the Bargate at 6.00 am by pupils of King Edward VI School

CHARLTON-ON-OTMOOR, Oxon
Church Garland ceremony

PADSTOW, Cornwall
May Day

**31st April – 3rd May**
MINEHEAD, Somerset
Whitecross at dawn on 1st May and Minehead in the evenings

**1st Saturday in May**
KNUTSFORD, Cheshire
Sanding and Royal May Day

**First weekend in May**
GAWTHORPE, nr Wakefield, West Yorkshire
May Day maypole celebration

**1st Sunday and second Saturday in May**
RANDWICK, nr Stroud, Gloucestershire
Randwick Wap, St John the Baptist's Church

**MAY DAY BANK HOLIDAY
(First Monday)**
ICKWELL Green, Bedfordshire
Ickwell May Day

ROCHESTER, Kent
Chimney sweeps' procession and Jack-in-the-Green.

HASTINGS, Kent
Jack-in-the-Green Festival, and Morris

WHITSTABLE, Kent
Jack-in-the-Green procession

**8th May (if Sunday or Monday then the Saturday before)**
HELSTON, Cornwall
Helston Furry Dance

**Early May**
LUSTLEIGH, Devon
May Queen

**13th May**
ABBOTSBURY, Dorset
Garland Day

**20th May (in 2006)**
Etwell, Derby
Well Dressing

**Ascension Eve**
WHITBY, North Yorkshire
Planting the Penny Hedge

TISSINGTON, Derbyshire
Well dressing at six wells

BISLEY, nr Stroud, Gloucestershire
Well blessing and garlands

OXFORD
Beating the Bounds of St Michael's
and hot penny scramble

LONDON, St George's Church, Borough of
Holborn
Beating the Bounds

LONDON, All Hallows at the tower
Beating the Bounds
TOWER OF LONDON
Beating the Bounds every 3 years
(2008, 2011)

**Whit Sunday**
BRIST0L
Rush Sunday at St Mary Redcliffe

ST BRIAVELS, Gloucestershire
Bread and cheese throwing

**Whit Monday**
ST IVES, Cambridgeshire
Dicing for Bibles Bequest

**Whit Friday**
SADDLEWORTH, Lancashire
Whit walks

**18th May (nearest Wednesday)**
NEWBIGGIN-BY-THE-SEA,
nr Morpeth, Northumberland
Dunting the Freeholder (Beating the Bounds)

**29th May – OAK APPLE DAY**
WISHFORD MAGNA, Wiltshire
Groveley Rights

CASTLETON, Derbyshire
Castleton Garland Day

**(or near)**
CHELSEA, London
Royal Hospital Founder's Day

WORCESTER
Royal Oak Apple Day

**SPRING BANK HOLIDAY**
BAMPTON, Oxon
Morris dancing and garlands

HEADINGTON, Oxon
Headington Quarry Morris Dancers in the
evening

COMBE MARTIN, North Devon
Hunting the Earl of Rone

COOPERS HILL, Birdlip, Gloucestershire
Cheese rolling

BARWICK-IN-ELMET, West Yorkshire
Maypole raising (every 3 years 2005,
2008, 2011)

**27th May (2006)**
ENDON, Staffordshire
Well dressing and crowning the May Queen

WIRKWORTH, Derbyshire
Well dressing (nine wells)

**Friday after Late Spring Bank Holiday**
CHIPPING CAMDEN, Gloucestershire
Cotswold Olympic Games, Dover's Hill

**Saturday after Late Spring Bank Holiday**
CHIPPING CAMDEN, Gloucestershire
The Scuttlebrook Wake

**(various dates in May or the
Spring Bank Holiday)**
CORBY, Northants
Corby Pole Fair
Every 20 years (next 2022, etc)

HAYES COMMON, Kent
May Queen of London Festival

ELSTOW ,Bedfordshire
May Festival

WELFORD-ON-AVON, Warwickshire
May Day Revels

WADWORTH, South Yorkshire
Maypole Dancing

OFFHAM, Kent;
MayDay

CHISLEHURST, Kent;
May Queen

HIGH WYCOMBE, Bucks
Weighing in the Mayor

WELLOW , near Ollerton Notts
May celebrations

# SELECTED READING

To date there has not been a single published work which gives a full survey of May events, but a bibliography covering the subject had been published by the EFDSS, also available on **www.efdss.org.uk**

The first large collection featuring May was made by John Brand in 1777. This was added to and reprinted at various times during the 19th century, culminating in W C Hazlitt's version in simplified dictionary form in 1905. Other works throughout the 19th century, including Chambers, Dyer, Ditchfield, Hone, Howitt and Strutt, amongst others, included the same or similar references.

The Folklore Society gathered this kind of published material into a single accessible form both as county and seasonal collections, most notably British Calendar Customs by A R Wright and T Lones. Other writers have similarly drawn from this stock of information. Chambers and Frazer were academic in intent, whereas Long and Whistler were more romantic and popular. Violet Alford and Christina Hole both try to present serious material in an easily understood form; Hutton is perhaps the best to date – not only drawing from all the previous publications but also from many historical references hitherto unpublished. Sykes and Shuel give photographic calendars of customs, together with some shrewd and unexpected comment on particular occasions. Benjamin Stone's photographs should also be mentioned in this context.

By far the best recent popular introductions are those by Hole and Shuel however these and many of the others cited below are now out of print.

Alford, Violet 1952 *Introduction to English Folklore*. London: G Bell

Brand, John 1813 *Observations on Popular Antiquities, etc*, additions by Henry Ellis, 2 vols. London: Rivington

Chambers, Robert (ed) 1863–4 *The Book of Days: A Miscellany of Popular Antiquities, in Connection With the Calendar*, 2 vols (Vol I). London & Edinburgh: W & R Chambers

Ditchfield, P H 1896 *British Customs Extant at the Present Time*. London: Redway

Dyer, T F T 1876 *British Popular Customs, Past and Present*. London: G Bell

Gutch (Mrs) (ed) 1899 *County Folk-Lore, Vol 2, Printed Extracts No 4, Examples of Printed Folk-Lore Concerning the North Riding of Yorkshire, York, and the Ainsty, collected and edited by Mrs Gutch.* London: David Nutt for the Folk-Lore Society

Gutch (Mrs) and Peacock, Mabel (eds) 1908 *County Folk-Lore, Vol 5, Printed Extracts No 7, Examples of Folk-Lore Concerning Lincolnshire, collected by Mrs Gutch and Mabel Peacock.* London: David Nutt for the Folk-Lore Society

Hazlitt, W Carew 1905 *Faiths and Folklore: A Dictionary of National Beliefs, Superstitions and Popular Customs...forming a New Edition of 'The Popular Antiquities of Great Britain',* 2 vols. London: Reeves & Turner

Hole, Christina Hole 1941–2 *English Custom and Usage.* London: Batsford

Hole, Christina 1976 *A Dictionary of British Folk Customs.* London: Hutchinson

Hone, William 1826–7 *Every-Day Book, etc,* 2 vols. London: Hunt & Clarke

Howitt, William 1838 *Rural Life in England,* 2 vols. London: Longman

Hunt, Cecil 1954 *British Customs and Ceremonies.* London: Ernest Benn

Hutton, Ronald 1996 *The Stations of the Sun.* Oxford: Oxford University Press

Knightley, Charles 1986 *The Customs and Ceremonies of Britain.* London:Thames & Hudson

Judge, Roy 1979 *The Jack-in-the-Green: a May Day custom.* London: Folklore Society

Long, George 1930 *The Folklore Calendar* London: Philip Allan

Rowe, Doc 1982 *We'll Call Once More Unto Your House.* Cornwall: Padstow Eko

Rowe, Doc & Robson, Carolyn 1993 *May: An Education Resource for the Summer Term on British Traditions.* 2 ed, ed M Taylor. London: EFDSS

Shuel, Brian 1985 *The National Trust Guide to Traditional Customs of Britain.* Exeter: Webb & Bower

Stone, Benjamin 1906 *Sir Benjamin Stone's Pictures: Records of National Life and Character,* 2 vols. London: Cassell

Sykes, Homer 1977 *Once a Year: some traditional British customs.* London: Gordon Fraser

Whistler, L 1947 *The English Festivals.* London: Heinemann

Wright, A R 1936–1940 *British Calendar Customs.* (3 vols, ed T Lones) London: William Glaisher

## OTHER SOURCES:

Doc Rowe Archive and collection
**www.docrowe.co.uk**

Folklore Society Library
**www.folklore-society.com**

National Centre for English Cultural Tradition
**www.shef.ac.uk/natcect**

RVW Memorial Library, English Folk Dance and Song Society
**www.edfss.org**

## PICTURE CREDITS:

All images © Doc Rowe except © Crown copyright. NMR: title page (CC72/00158);
27 (CC73/00632); 37 (CC73/01432); 83 (CC72/00175)